PIANO
Adventures *by Nancy and Randall Faber*
A BASIC PIANO METHOD

CONTENTS

About the "Sightreading Stocking Stuffers"

A student's enthusiasm for learning Christmas music can become an opportunity to create enthusiasm for sightreading. In this book, each Christmas song is presented with short melodies, called "Sightreading Stocking Stuffers."

The "Sightreading Stocking Stuffers" are **melodic variations** of the carol being studied. Through repetition of familiar rhythmic and melodic patterns, the student begins to build a visual and aural musical vocabulary.

The "stocking stuffers" provide opportunity for transposition, reinforcing theory, and musicianship skills.

The student should sightread one "stocking stuffer" a day while learning the Christmas song. Or, the stocking stuffers can be used as sightreading during the lesson itself.

The teacher may wish to tell the student:

> **Sightreading means "reading music at first sight."**
>
> When sightreading, music is not practiced over and over. Instead, it is only played several times with the highest concentration.

The following **3 C's** may help the student with sightreading:

CORRECT HAND POSITION
Find the correct starting note for each hand.
Scan the music for rhythmic and melodic patterns.

COUNT - OFF
Set a steady tempo by counting one "free" measure
before starting to play.

CONCENTRATE
Focus your eyes on the music, carefully reading the intervals.
Remember to keep your eyes moving ahead!

Note to Teacher: This page reviews theory concepts in the major keys of C, G, F, and D and the minor keys of Am and Dm. This will help prepare the student for the carols and sightreading that follow.

Stuffing the Stockings

Draw a line connecting each "gift" to the correct stocking.

Silent Night

Words by Joseph Mohr
Music by Franz Grüber

FF

Sightread one "stocking stuffer" a day
while learning the carol. Your teacher
may also ask you to transpose.

Circle the stocking after sightreading!

PEACEFUL STOCKING STUFFERS

("variations" for sightreading)

Can you transpose to D major?

Can you transpose to G major?
(R.H. fingers 1-3 begin on B and D.)

Can you transpose to F major?

DAY 5 In *Silent Night,* circle each
left-hand **octave.**

Hint: There are 5.

DAY 6 In *Silent Night,* put a ✔ above
each right-hand **6th.**

Hint: There are 7.

Toyland
(from the operetta *Babes in Toyland*)

Words by Glen MacDonough
Music by Victor Herbert

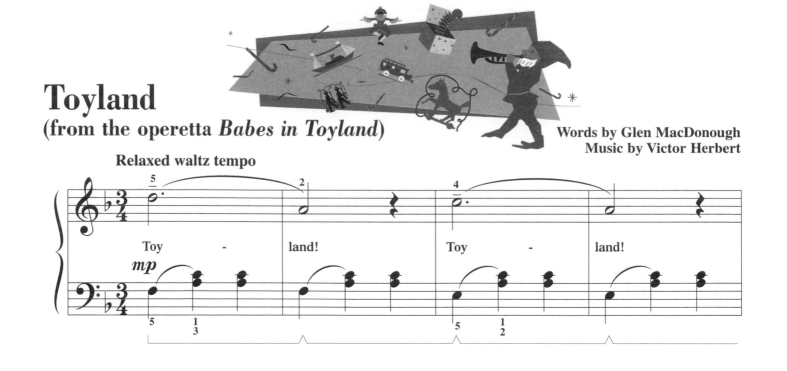

Relaxed waltz tempo

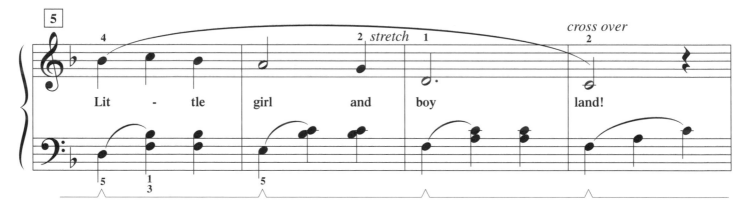

Toy - land! Toy - land!

Lit - tle girl and boy land!

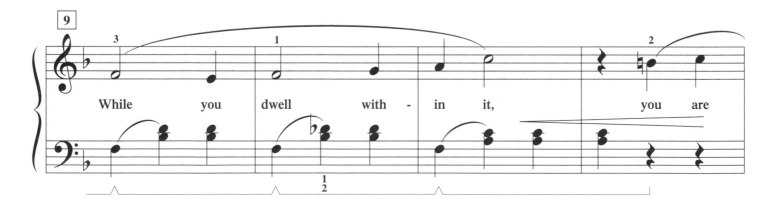

While you dwell with - in it, you are

ev - er hap - py then.

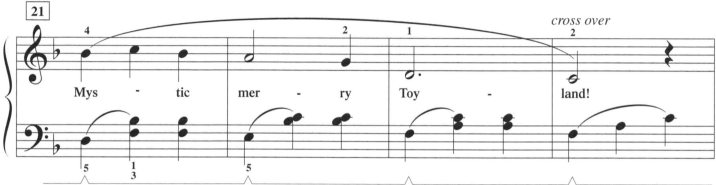

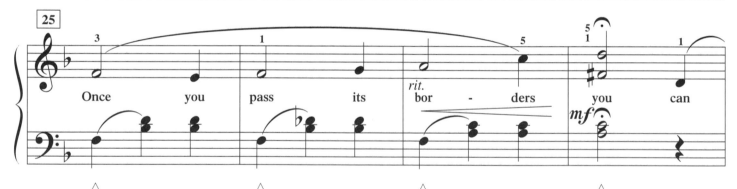

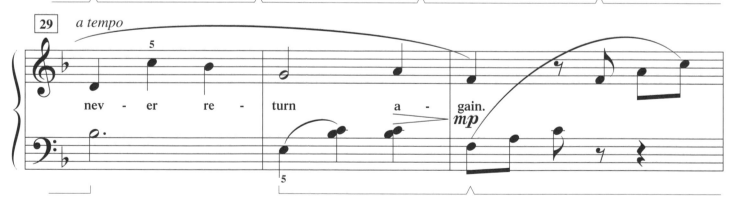

Sightread one "stocking stuffer" a day while learning *Toyland.*

Circle the stocking after sightreading!

("variations" for sightreading)

(R.H. finger 5 begins on E.)

DAY 1

Can you transpose to C major?
(L.H. finger 1 begins on A.)

DAY 2

Can you transpose to G major?

DAY 3

Hint: Keep eyes moving ahead to prepare each L.H. chord!

DAY 4

DAY 5 Name the correct step of the scale for each note below: **1 2 3 4 5 6** or **7.**

scale step   **6**
Ex.

DAY 6 Put a ✔ above the 3 measures that use a **V7 waltz chord** in F major.

8

FF1

Coventry Carol
(Theme and Variation)

Theme

Traditional English Carol

Rather slowly, gently

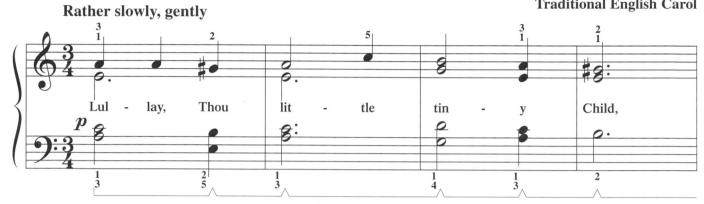

Lul - lay, Thou lit - tle tin - y Child,

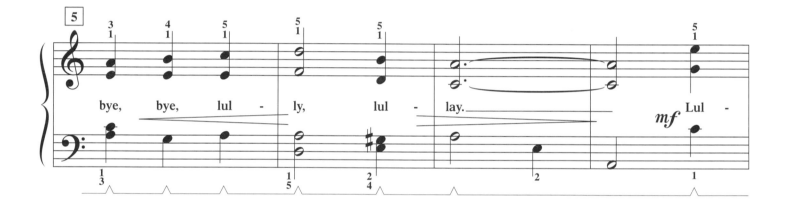

bye, bye, lul - ly, lul - lay. ____ *mf* Lul -

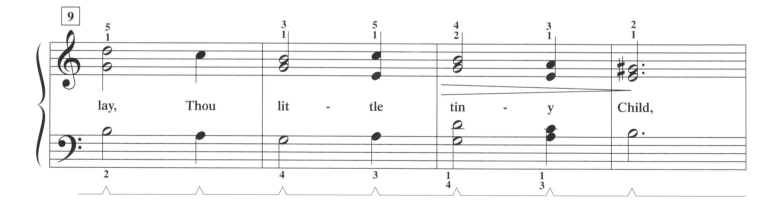

lay, Thou lit - tle tin - y Child,

bye, bye, lul - ly lul - lay. ____ *pp*

Variation

Sightread one "stocking stuffer" a day
while learning *Coventry Carol.*

Circle the stocking after sightreading!

COVENTRY STOCKING STUFFERS

("variations" for sightreading)

Can you transpose to D minor?

The **theme** and **variation**
end in A major.

True or False
(*circle one*)

Can you play the **L.H. alone**
of the *theme* while your R.H.
taps **beats 1, 2,** and **3** on your lap?

God Rest Ye Merry, Gentlemen

Traditional English Carol

With vigor

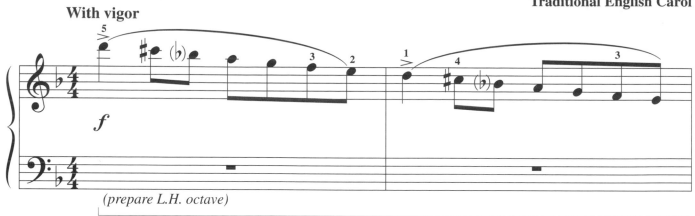

(prepare L.H. octave)

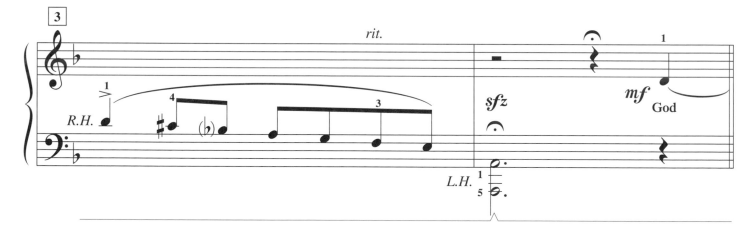

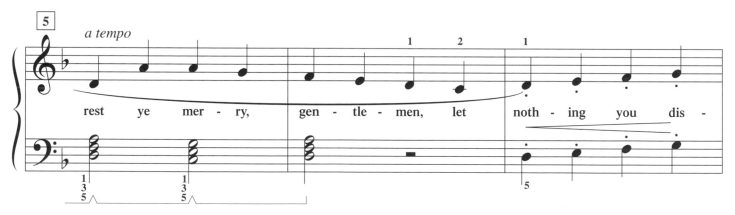

FF

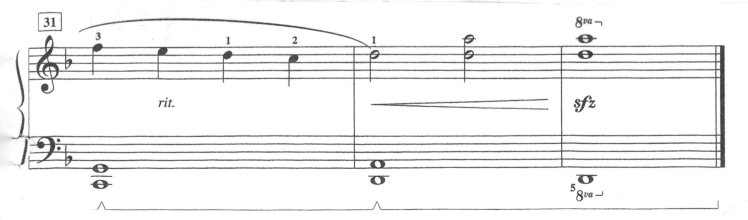

Silent Night
Level Two

Franz Gruber
Arr. Gilbert DeBenedetti

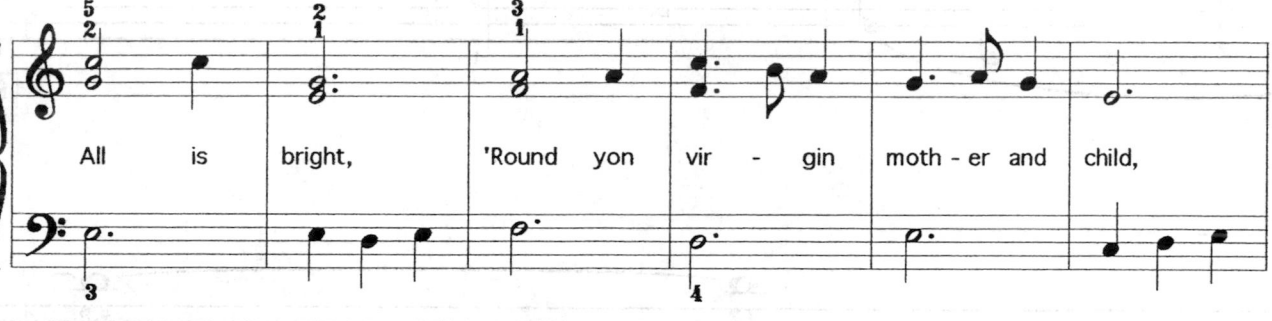

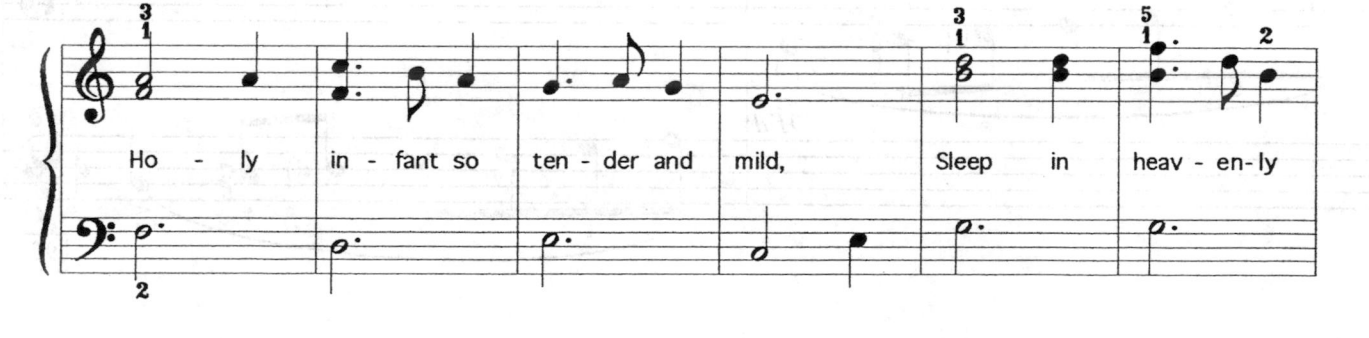

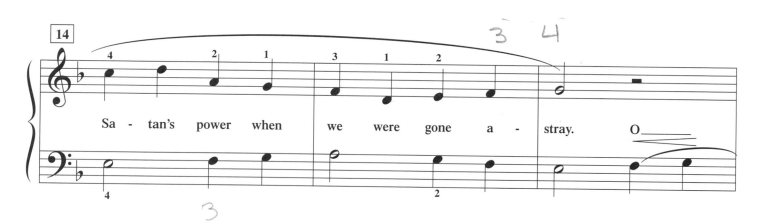

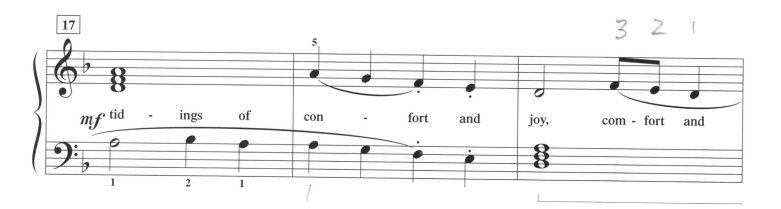

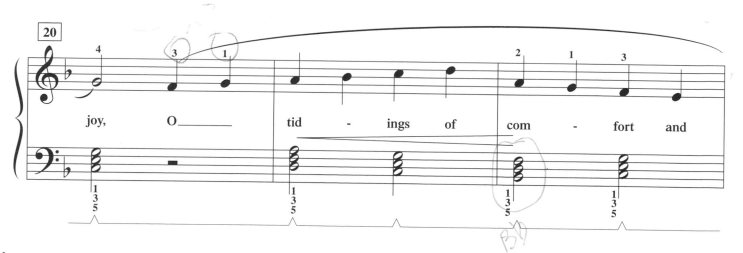

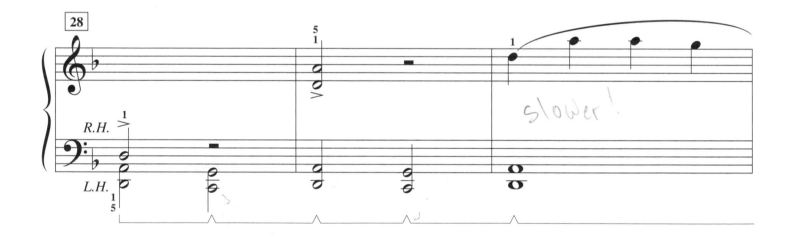

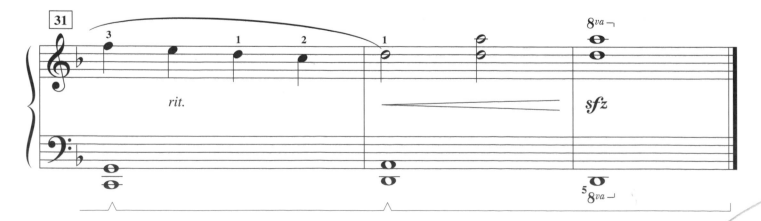

Sightread one "stocking stuffer" a day
while learning *God Rest Ye Merry, Gentlemen.*

Circle the stocking after sightreading!

("variations" for sightreading)

Joy to the World

With joy, not too fast

Words by Isaac Watts
Music by George Frideric Handel

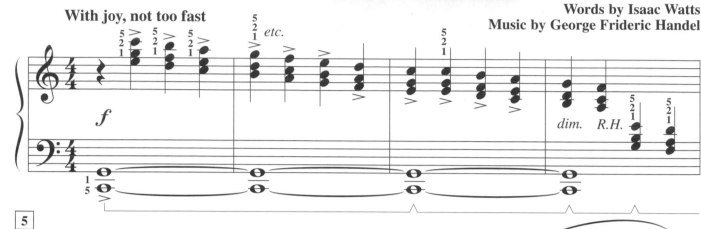

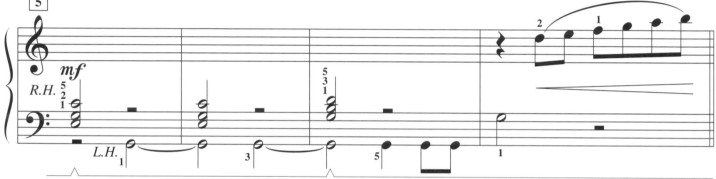

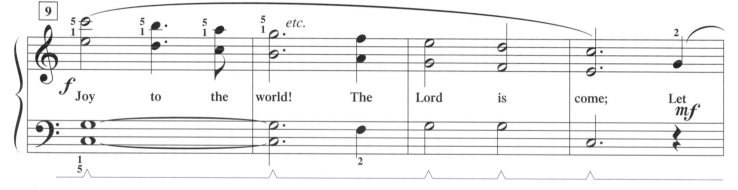

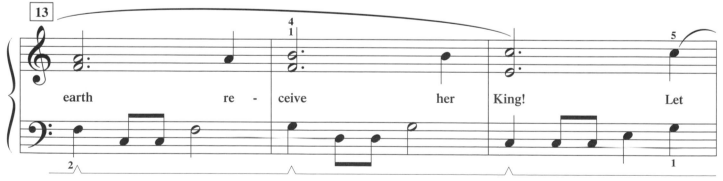

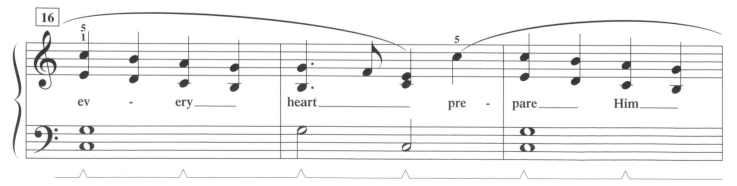

16

FF12

room,_____ and heav'n and na - ture____ sing, and____

mp *mf*

heav'n and na - ture____ sing, and____ heav'n____ and

f

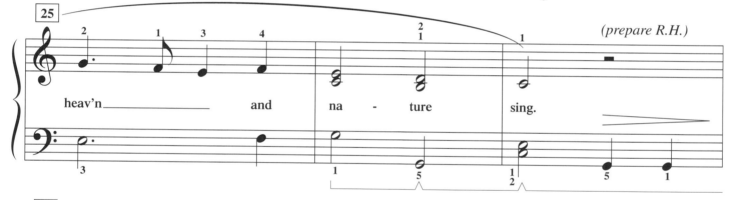

heav'n_____ and na - ture sing.

(prepare R.H.)

mp

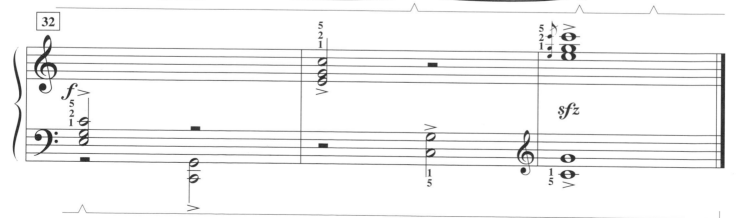

f *sfz*

JOYOUS STOCKING STUFFERS

("variations" for sightreading)

Sightread one "stocking stuffer" a day while learning *Joy to the World.*

Circle the stocking after sightreading!

Can you transpose to D major?

DAY 1

f-p on repeat

Can you transpose to G major?

DAY 2

p

Can you transpose to G major?

DAY 3

f   *rit.*

Can you transpose to F major?

DAY 4

mf

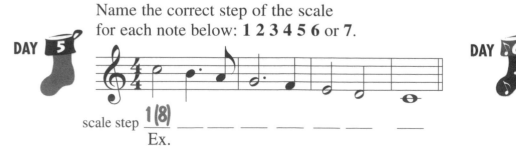

DAY 5

Name the correct step of the scale for each note below: **1 2 3 4 5 6** or **7**.

scale step **1 (8)** ___ ___ ___ ___ ___ ___
Ex.

DAY 6

Put a ✔ above each measure of the carol that uses only notes of the **C major chord**.

Hint: There are 8.

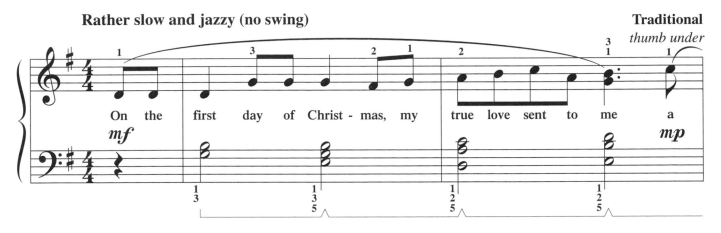

The Twelve Days of Christmas

Rather slow and jazzy (no swing)

Traditional

thumb under

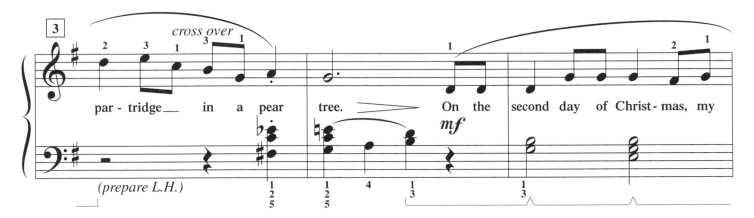

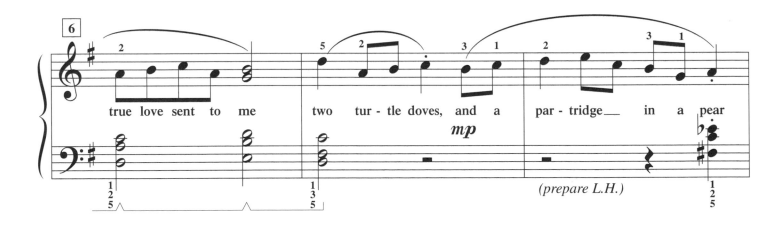

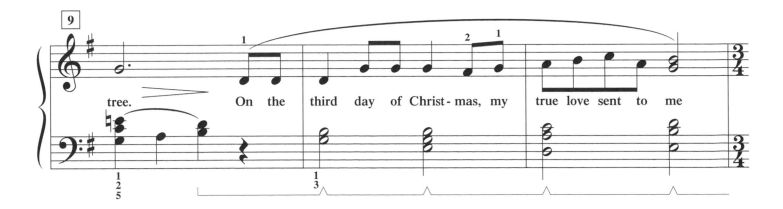

12

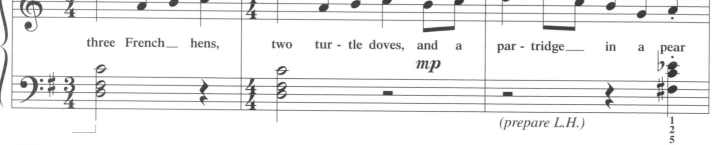

three French_ hens,   two tur - tle doves, and a   *mp*   par - tridge_ in a pear

(prepare L.H.)

15

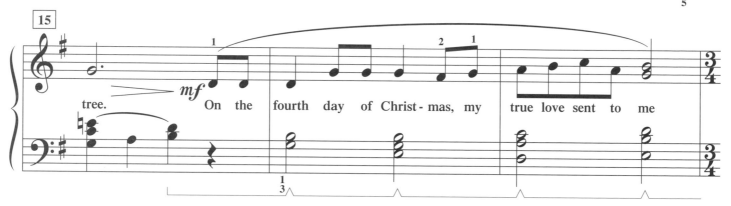

tree.   *mf*   On the   fourth day of Christ - mas, my   true love sent to me

18

four call - ing birds,
three French_ hens,   two tur - tle doves and a   *mp*   par - tridge_ in a pear

21

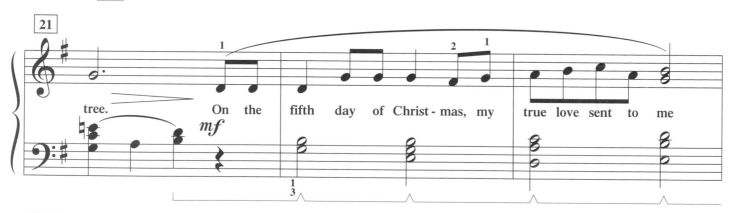

tree.   On the   fifth day of Christ - mas, my   true love sent to me

24

f five   gold_   rings,   *mf*   four_ call - ing birds,   three French hens,

20

Sightread one "stocking stuffer" a day
while learning *The Twelve Days of Christmas.*

Circle the stocking after sightreading!

("variations" for sightreading)

Hint: Watch the R.H. fingering carefully!

FF1

What two key signatures are used in this "stocking stuffer?" _____: 1 flat

_____: 1 sharp

DAY 3

Rather slowly

cross over

mp

mf

3

cross over

DAY 4

Rather slowly

mf

3

rit.

DAY 5 Circle six **E minor chords** for the L.H. in this piece.

DAY 6 Name the correct step of the scale for each note below: **1 2 3 4 5 6** or **7.**

scale step **5** ___ ___ ___ ___ ___
Ex.

Hallelujah Chorus
(from Handel's *Messiah*)

George Frideric Handel

With joy

Hal - le - lu - jah! Hal - le - lu - jah! Hal - le -

lu - jah! Hal - le - lu - jah! Hal - le - lu - jah!

Hal - le - lu - jah! Hal - le - lu - jah! Hal - le -

lu - jah! Hal - le - lu - jah! Hal - le - lu - jah!

FF1

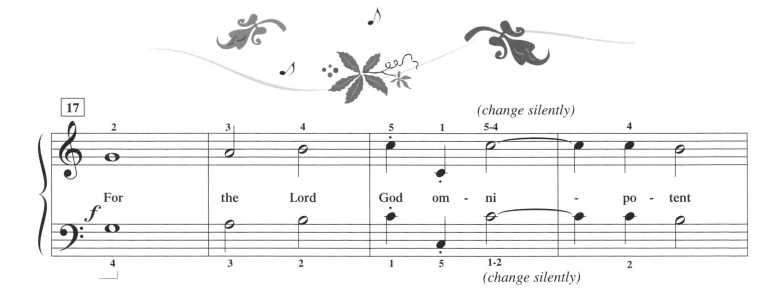

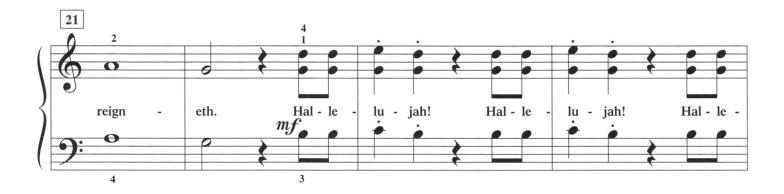

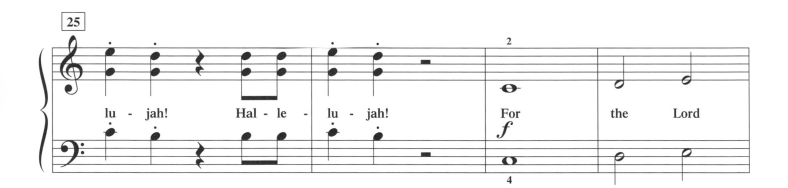

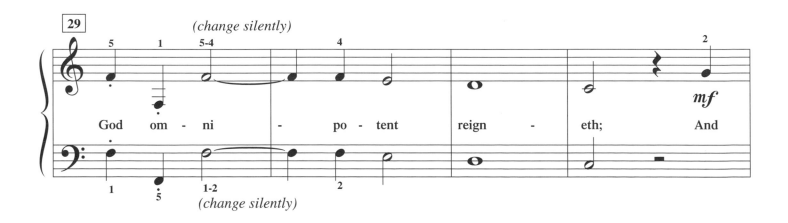

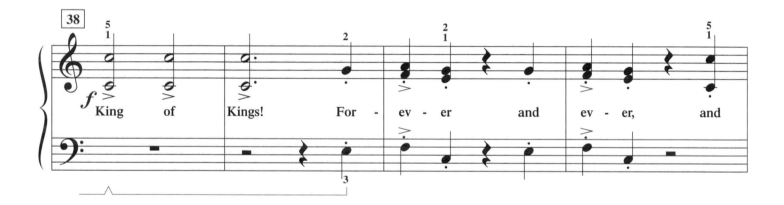

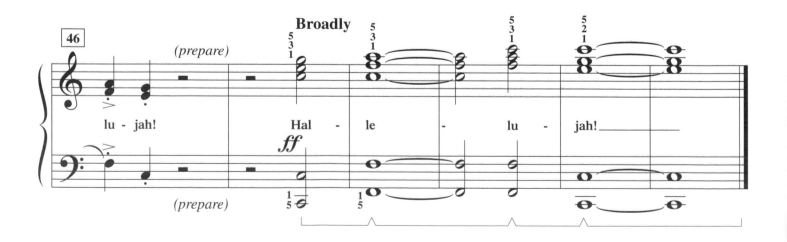

Sightread one "stocking stuffer" a day
while learning the *Hallelujah Chorus.*

Circle the stocking after sightreading!

("variations" for sightreading)

First name the intervals in measures 1-2.

Parade of the Tin Soldiers

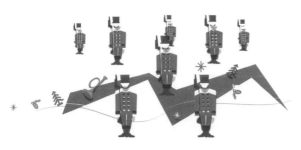

Leon Jessel

Brightly

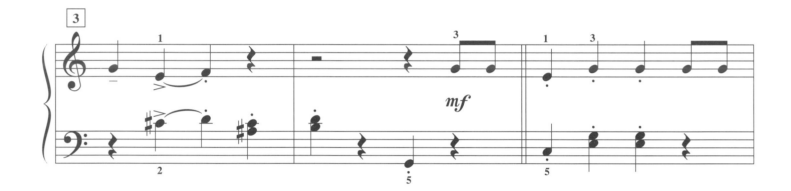

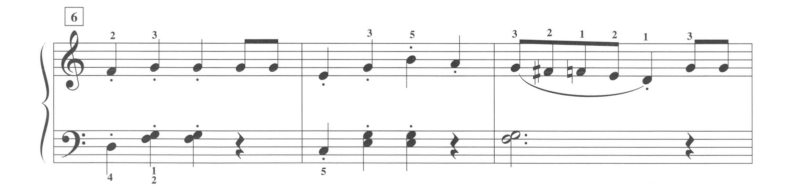

FF1

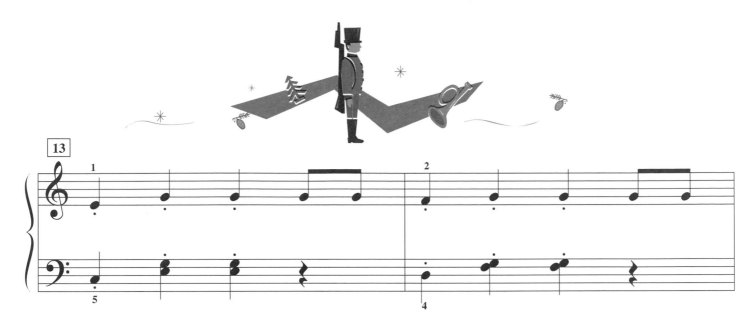

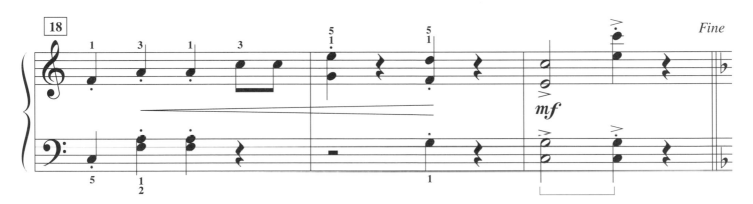

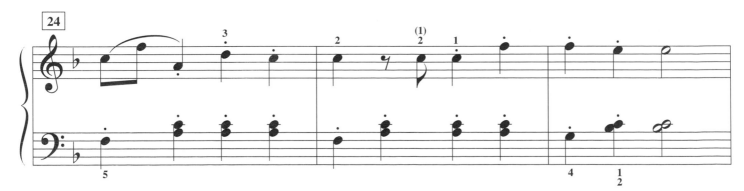

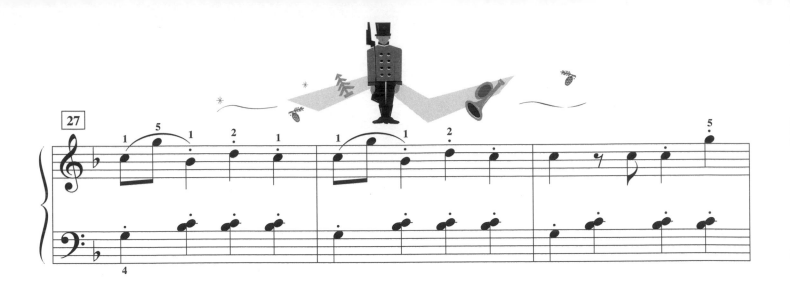

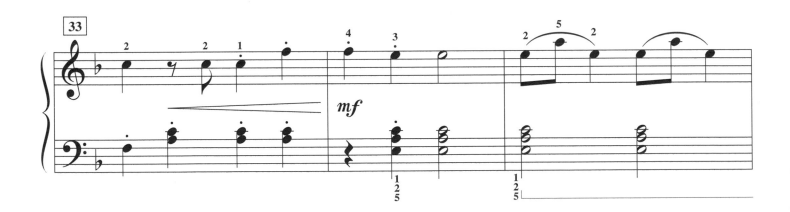

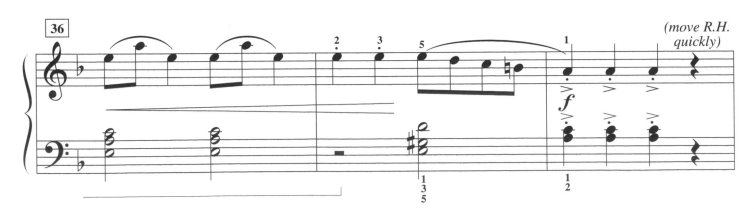

FF

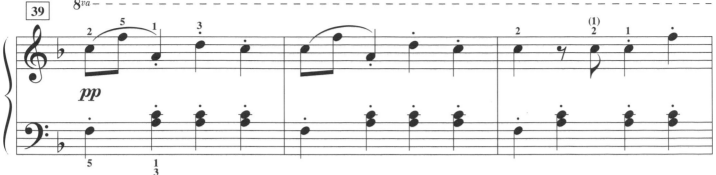

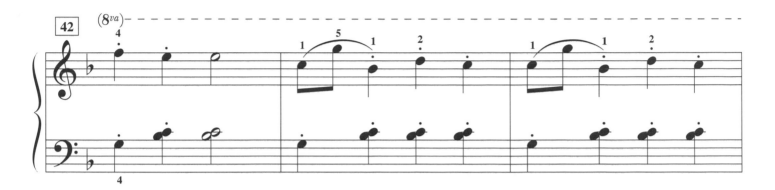

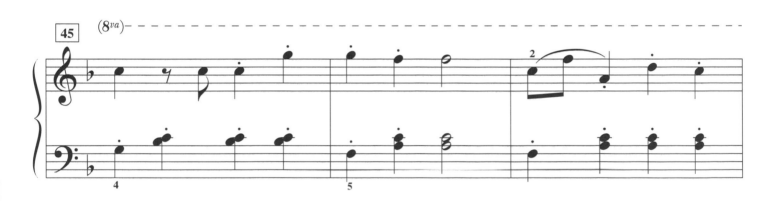

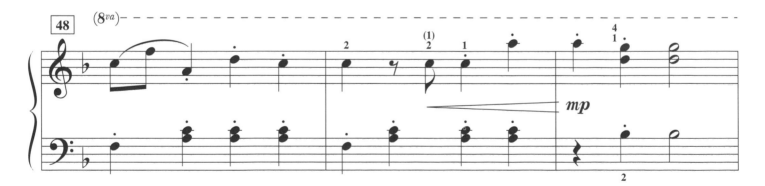

D.C. al Fine

Sightread one "stocking stuffer" a day while learning *Parade of the Tin Soldiers.*

Circle the stocking after sightreading!

("variations" for sightreading)

DAY 1

DAY 2

DAY 3

DAY 4

DAY 5 — Where does *Parade of the Tin Soldiers* change to a new key? *measure* _____

Write the new key name in the music.

DAY 6 — In *measure 8* the R.H. plays a **descending** (moving down) pattern of 8th notes.

Where does the L.H. play an **ascending** (moving up) pattern of 8th notes? *measure* _____

FF1